THE COST OF THESE DREAMS

Sports Stories and Other Serious Business

WRIGHT THOMPSON

Published by 535
An imprint of Blink Publishing
The Plaza, 535 Kings Road,
Chelsea Harbour,
London, SW10 0SZ

www.blinkpublishing.co.uk

facebook.com/blinkpublishing
twitter.com/blinkpublishing

Trade Paperback – 9781788701969
eBook – 9781788701976

A CIP catalogue of this book is available from the British Library.

Printed and bound by Clays Ltd, Elcograf S.p.A.

1 3 5 7 9 10 8 6 4 2

Blink Publishing is an imprint of the Bonnier Publishing Group
www.bonnierpublishing.co.uk